City and Country Homes

Debbie Gallagher

MACMILLAN

Y

Trinity Grammar School
Junior School
Lewisham

First published in 2007 by
MACMILLAN EDUCATION AUSTRALIA PTY LTD
627 Chapel Street, South Yarra 3141

Visit our website at www.macmillan.com.au or go directly to www.macmillanlibrary.com.au

Associated companies and representatives throughout the world.

Copyright © Debbie Gallagher 2007

National Library of Australia
Cataloguing-in-Publication data

Gallagher, Debbie, 1969– .
 City and country homes.

 Includes index.
 For primary school children.
 ISBN 978 1 4202 0565 7.
 ISBN 1 4202 0565 X.

 1. Dwellings – Juvenile literature. 2. Country homes –
 Juvenile literature. 3. Architecture, Domestic – Juvenile
 literature. I. Title. (Series: Macmillan young library.
 Homes around the world).

728

Edited by Angelique Campbell-Muir
Text and cover design by Christine Deering
Page layout by Domenic Lauricella
Photo research by Legend Images
Illustration by Domenic Lauricella

Printed in China

Acknowledgements

The author and the publisher are grateful to the following for permission to reproduce copyright material:

Cover photograph: Semi-detached home © Barry Mason/Alamy.

© Education Photos/Alamy, p. 15; © Richard Levine/Alamy, p. 10; © Barry Mason/Alamy, pp. 1, 13; © Coo-ee Picture
Library, p. 20; © Aaleksander/Dreamstime.com, pp. 7 (bottom), 24; © Breck/Dreamstime.com, p. 30 (centre left);
© Brownm39Dreamstime.com, p. 30 (bottom right); © Elenathewise/Dreamstime.com, pp. 6 (centre), 12;
© Gbphotostock/Dreamstime.com, p. 14; © iStockphoto.com, p. 23; © iStockphoto.com/Eric Bechtold, pp. 8, 30 (top
right); © iStockphoto.com/Jacques Croizer, p. 30 (top left); © iStockphoto.com/Narelle Robson-Petch, pp. 7 (top), 22;
© iStockphoto.com/eva serrabassa, pp. 6 (top), 9; © iStockphoto.com/Daniella Zalcman, pp. 3, 11; © Lonely Planet
Images/Mark Daffey, p. 4; © Mark Moxon, www.moxon.net, p. 30 (bottom left); © Michael Spencer/Saudi Aramco World/
PADIA, p. 30 (centre right); © Photolibrary/Jtb Photo Communications Inc., pp. 6 (bottom), 16, 25, 27; © Photolibrary/
Panorama Media (Beijing) Ltd., pp. 17, 18; © Photolibrary/Robert Harding Picture Library Ltd., p. 21; © Photos.com, p. 5;
© KIN CHEUNG/Reuters/Picture Media, p. 19; © Wikipedia, p. 26.

While every care has been taken to trace and acknowledge copyright, the publisher tenders their apologies for any
accidental infringement where copyright has proved untraceable. Where the attempt has been unsuccessful, the
publisher welcomes information that would redress the situation.

This Book was purchased with funds provided by:
The Australian Federal Government
JOSD Grant 2007

Contents

Glossary words

When a word is printed in **bold**, you can look up its meaning in the Glossary on page 31.

Shelter

Everyone needs shelter, as well as food and water, warmth and protection. Homes around the world provide shelter for people.

Cities are places where lots of people live close together.

People live in many different types of homes. In cities, people build their homes close together. In the **countryside**, homes have more space around them.

Farmers sometimes use the space around their homes to raise their animals.

City and country homes

City homes come in many different shapes and sizes. In cities, the two most common types of homes are houses and apartments.

Different homes in the same building are called apartments.

A city home that is joined to just one other home is called a semi-detached home.

The Hakka people build their apartment homes inside a circular wall.

Country homes have a lot of land around them.
People can grow crops for food and raise animals.

Queenslander houses are built in both the city and the country.

Minka farmhouses are a special type of home found in Japan.

New York City apartment

Most people in New York City live in apartments. They are homes for single people as well as for families.

Apartment buildings can have many homes on each level.

Apartment buildings are made of brick or stone.
Stairs or **elevators** are used to travel between the
different levels.

different apartments

fire escape stairs

New York City apartments have fire escapes on the outside of the building.

Inside a New York City apartment

Inside a New York City apartment the kitchen is usually small. There is a living room for relaxing or entertaining guests. There may be one or more bedrooms, and a bathroom.

cupboards and drawers for storage

doorway to outside the apartment

doorway to other rooms

Apartment kitchens fit a lot of things into a small space.

Apartments allow a lot of people to live in the one area. This means people can live close to shops and close to work.

Tens of thousands of people live on Manhattan Island in New York.

English semi-detached home

When two houses are built joined together they are called semi-detached homes. This type of home is popular in city suburbs in England.

The two sides of a semi-detached home have the same shape.

Because semi-detached homes share a wall, they cost less to build. They can be made of brick, stone or wood. Each room has at least one window to let in light.

home 1   shared wall   home 2

windows

windows

front doors

front gardens

Semi-detached homes can have more than one level.

Inside an English semi-detached home

Inside a semi-detached home there is a kitchen and a bathroom. There is a family living area and separate bedrooms.

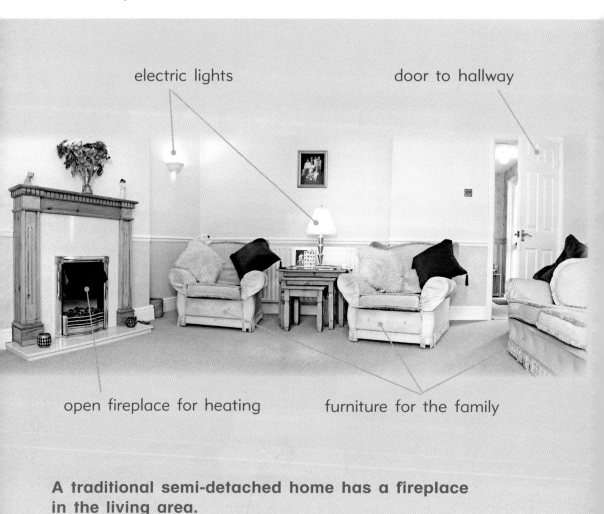

electric lights

door to hallway

open fireplace for heating

furniture for the family

A traditional semi-detached home has a fireplace in the living area.

A semi-detached home has more space than an apartment. Children can play in the garden around the house.

Most semi-detached homes have a front and a back garden.

Round earth building

Round earth buildings are built by the Hakka people in country areas of China. Each building is divided into apartments.

There are about 20 families living inside each round earth building.

Most Hakka homes are made of earth or mud. Some are made of stone or bricks. There is a **courtyard** in the middle of each round building.

sloped roof

windows on upper level

courtyard

windows on middle level

The Hakka have lived in round earth homes for over 500 years.

Inside a round earth building

There are three levels inside a round earth building. Each apartment has a room on each level. The lower-level room is for cooking and the top is for sleeping.

three levels

doorway into central courtyard

apartment doorway

Families use their middle-level room to store things.

Round earth buildings have few windows around the outside. Windows on the upper floor are small. There are no windows on the lower floor.

Children can play outside the round earth buildings.

Queenslander home

The Queenslander home is a **traditional** home found in Queensland, Australia. Queenslander houses are raised on stumps.

Stumps can be as high as two metres.

Queensland can get very hot. The homes are raised so that air can flow freely beneath and around the home. These cooling breezes help to keep the homes cool.

sloping corrugated iron roof

windows

house stumps

front entrance stairs

Trees around the home provide shade from the Sun.

Inside a Queenslander home

Inside a Queenslander home there are bedrooms and a living area. Doors and windows open to let cool breezes blow through. Steps lead up to the front door

front door

verandah

windows

Many Queenslander homes have verandahs for shade.

The space under the house can be used for different things. Children can play under the house. When it is raining clothes can be hung there to dry.

Some houses are so high off the ground a person can stand underneath.

Minka farmhouse

Minka farmhouses are found in the countryside of Japan. They are designed and built according to very old traditions.

The land around a minka farmhouse is used for growing food and raising animals.

Minka farmhouses are made out of wood. The roof is covered with **thatch** or **shingles**. In areas where it snows the roofs have steep sides.

It is easier for the snow to slide off the sloped roofs.

Inside a minka farmhouse

Inside a minka farmhouse there are two sections. One section has a raised wooden floor with a fireplace and a ceiling above. Around the sides are rooms for sleeping.

The fireplace is used to make tea, an important ceremony in Japan.

The second section has a hard earth floor. The inside of the roof can be seen above.

Outside, shingle roofs are decorated with wooden carvings.

Floor plan

This is a **floor plan** of a New York City apartment. It gives you a 'bird's eye view' of the layout of the areas inside.

Apartment 1

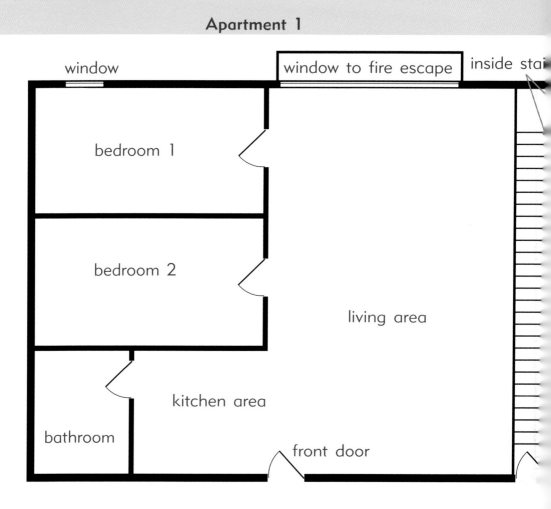

window

window to fire escape

inside stai

bedroom 1

bedroom 2

living area

kitchen area

bathroom

front door

Try this!

Draw a floor plan of your home. Label all the spaces, inside and outside, as well as features like doors and windows.

Apartment 2

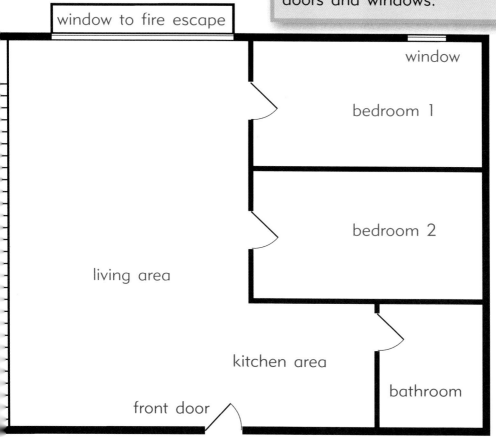

window to fire escape

window

bedroom 1

bedroom 2

living area

kitchen area

bathroom

front door

Homes around the world

There are many different types of homes around the world. All homes provide shelter and other things needed by the people who live in them.

Pit home in Africa

New York City apartments

Windsor Castle in London

Mud and grass homes

Tuareg tent in the Sahara Desert

Lake home in Asia

Glossary

countryside   the rural part of a country, outside cities and towns, where there are farms

courtyard   an outside area enclosed by walls or buildings

elevators   moving platforms or cages that take people between different floors in a building

floor plan   a drawing showing the layout of the areas in a home or building, as if seen from above

shingles   thin pieces of wood that overlap each other to cover the roof and sides of a house

thatch   grass, straw or leaves, often used as a roof covering

traditional   used for a long time by a particular people or in a particular area

Index